50 Simple Dishes for the Solo Cook Recipes

By: Kelly Johnson

Table of Contents

- One-Pan Lemon Garlic Chicken
- Spaghetti Aglio e Olio
- Quick Veggie Stir-Fry
- Grilled Cheese and Tomato Soup
- Sheet Pan Salmon and Veggies
- Scrambled Eggs with Spinach
- Easy Chicken Fajitas
- Rice and Bean Burrito Bowl
- Simple Shrimp Scampi
- Quinoa and Avocado Salad
- One-Pot Pasta Primavera
- Teriyaki Chicken Stir-Fry
- Baked Sweet Potato with Toppings
- Pesto Zucchini Noodles
- Chicken Caesar Salad
- Classic Tuna Salad Sandwich
- Egg Fried Rice
- Veggie and Hummus Wrap
- One-Skillet Beef and Broccoli
- Avocado Toast with Poached Egg
- Chicken and Rice Soup
- Mushroom Risotto
- Turkey and Swiss Quesadilla
- Grilled Chicken with Mixed Greens
- Homemade Mac and Cheese
- Spinach and Feta Stuffed Chicken
- Lentil and Vegetable Stew
- Baked Chicken Parmesan
- Tofu and Vegetable Stir-Fry
- Omelette with Mushrooms and Cheese
- BBQ Chicken Salad
- Spicy Peanut Noodles
- Sausage and Bell Pepper Skillet
- Greek Salad with Grilled Chicken
- Tomato Basil Pasta

- Cottage Pie for One
- Eggplant Parmesan
- Garlic Butter Shrimp with Rice
- Pulled Pork Tacos
- Chickpea Curry
- Mini Meatloaf
- Turkey Chili
- Baked Cod with Lemon
- Sautéed Brussels Sprouts with Bacon
- Pancakes for One
- Grilled Veggie Sandwich
- Creamy Chicken Alfredo
- Spinach and Ricotta Stuffed Peppers
- Steak and Potato Skillet
- Broccoli and Cheddar Frittata

One-Pan Lemon Garlic Chicken

Ingredients:

- 4 boneless, skinless chicken breasts
- 1 lemon (zested and juiced)
- 4 garlic cloves, minced
- 1 tbsp olive oil
- 1/2 cup chicken broth
- 1 tbsp butter
- Salt and pepper to taste
- 1 tsp dried oregano or thyme
- Fresh parsley for garnish (optional)

Instructions:

1. **Preheat the oven** to 400°F (200°C).
2. **Season the chicken** breasts on both sides with salt, pepper, and oregano (or thyme).
3. **Sear the chicken**: Heat olive oil in a large oven-safe skillet over medium-high heat. Add chicken breasts and cook for 4-5 minutes on each side, until golden brown. Remove and set aside.
4. **Prepare the lemon garlic sauce**: In the same skillet, add minced garlic and cook for about 1 minute until fragrant. Pour in chicken broth, lemon juice, and lemon zest. Stir to combine.
5. **Add the chicken back** to the skillet. Spoon some of the lemon garlic sauce over the top of the chicken.
6. **Bake** in the preheated oven for 15-20 minutes, or until the chicken is fully cooked (internal temperature should reach 165°F).
7. **Finish with butter**: After baking, remove the skillet from the oven and stir in the butter to create a silky sauce.
8. **Serve and garnish**: Serve the chicken with the sauce drizzled over the top and garnish with fresh parsley if desired.

This flavorful one-pan recipe makes a perfect weeknight dinner, with minimal cleanup and maximum taste!

Spaghetti Aglio e Olio

Ingredients:

- 12 oz spaghetti
- 1/4 cup olive oil
- 6 garlic cloves, thinly sliced
- 1/4 tsp red pepper flakes (optional)
- Salt to taste
- Fresh parsley, chopped
- Parmesan cheese (optional)

Instructions:

Cook the spaghetti according to package instructions. Reserve 1 cup of pasta water and drain the rest. Heat olive oil in a large skillet over medium heat. Add the garlic slices and red pepper flakes, sautéing until golden and fragrant (about 2 minutes). Toss in the spaghetti and mix well to coat in the garlic oil. Add some reserved pasta water to achieve desired consistency. Season with salt, toss with chopped parsley, and serve with grated Parmesan if desired.

Quick Veggie Stir-Fry

Ingredients:

- 1 tbsp sesame oil
- 1 bell pepper, sliced
- 1 carrot, thinly sliced
- 1 zucchini, sliced
- 1 cup broccoli florets
- 2 garlic cloves, minced
- 2 tbsp soy sauce
- 1 tsp honey or maple syrup
- 1 tsp sesame seeds (optional)

Instructions:

Heat sesame oil in a large pan over medium heat. Add garlic and sauté for 1 minute. Add vegetables (bell pepper, carrot, zucchini, broccoli) and stir-fry for 5-7 minutes until tender but still crisp. Drizzle with soy sauce and honey (or maple syrup), tossing to coat. Cook for an additional 1-2 minutes. Garnish with sesame seeds and serve over rice or noodles.

Grilled Cheese and Tomato Soup

Ingredients for Grilled Cheese:

- 4 slices of bread
- 2 tbsp butter
- 4 slices cheddar cheese

Ingredients for Tomato Soup:

- 2 tbsp olive oil
- 1 small onion, diced
- 2 garlic cloves, minced
- 1 can (28 oz) crushed tomatoes
- 1 cup vegetable broth
- 1 tsp sugar
- Salt and pepper to taste
- Fresh basil (optional)

Instructions:

For Grilled Cheese: Butter one side of each bread slice. Heat a skillet over medium heat, place one slice butter-side down, top with cheese, and cover with the other slice (butter-side up). Grill each side for 2-3 minutes until golden and crispy.
For Tomato Soup: Sauté onion and garlic in olive oil in a pot over medium heat until soft (about 5 minutes). Add crushed tomatoes, vegetable broth, sugar, salt, and pepper. Bring to a simmer and cook for 10-15 minutes. Blend if desired for a smooth texture, and garnish with fresh basil. Enjoy this classic comfort meal!

Sheet Pan Salmon and Veggies

Ingredients:

- 4 salmon fillets
- 1 lb baby potatoes, halved
- 1 lb asparagus, trimmed
- 2 tbsp olive oil
- 1 lemon, sliced
- 2 garlic cloves, minced
- Salt and pepper to taste
- Fresh parsley for garnish (optional)

Instructions:

Preheat the oven to 400°F (200°C). Toss baby potatoes with 1 tbsp olive oil, garlic, salt, and pepper. Spread on a sheet pan and roast for 15 minutes. Remove the pan, add asparagus, toss with the remaining olive oil, and place the salmon fillets on the sheet. Season the salmon with salt, pepper, and lemon slices. Roast for an additional 10-12 minutes until the salmon is cooked through. Garnish with fresh parsley if desired.

Scrambled Eggs with Spinach

Ingredients:

- 4 eggs
- 1 cup fresh spinach, chopped
- 1 tbsp butter
- Salt and pepper to taste
- 1 tbsp milk (optional)

Instructions:

Whisk the eggs with salt, pepper, and milk if using. Heat butter in a non-stick pan over medium heat. Add the spinach and cook for 1 minute until wilted. Pour in the eggs and cook, stirring constantly, until scrambled and cooked through. Serve immediately.

Easy Chicken Fajitas

Ingredients:

- 2 chicken breasts, sliced into thin strips
- 1 bell pepper, sliced
- 1 onion, sliced
- 1 tbsp olive oil
- 1 tbsp fajita seasoning
- Flour tortillas
- Optional toppings: sour cream, guacamole, salsa

Instructions:

Heat olive oil in a skillet over medium-high heat. Add the chicken strips and cook until browned, about 5 minutes. Add the bell pepper, onion, and fajita seasoning, cooking for another 5-7 minutes until the veggies are soft. Serve in flour tortillas with your choice of toppings.

Rice and Bean Burrito Bowl

Ingredients:

- 1 cup cooked rice
- 1 can black beans, drained and rinsed
- 1/2 cup corn kernels
- 1/2 cup diced tomatoes
- 1/4 cup shredded cheddar cheese
- 1 avocado, sliced
- 1 tbsp lime juice
- 1 tsp cumin
- Salt and pepper to taste
- Fresh cilantro for garnish (optional)

Instructions:

In a bowl, layer the cooked rice, black beans, corn, and diced tomatoes. Sprinkle with cumin, lime juice, salt, and pepper. Top with shredded cheese, avocado slices, and fresh cilantro. Serve immediately.

Simple Shrimp Scampi

Ingredients:

- 1 lb shrimp, peeled and deveined
- 4 garlic cloves, minced
- 1/4 cup butter
- 1/4 cup white wine or chicken broth
- 1 tbsp lemon juice
- 1 tbsp olive oil
- Salt and pepper to taste
- Fresh parsley for garnish

Instructions:

Heat olive oil and butter in a skillet over medium heat. Add the garlic and sauté for 1 minute. Add the shrimp, cooking until pink (about 2-3 minutes per side). Pour in the wine (or broth) and lemon juice, simmering for another minute. Season with salt and pepper, and garnish with fresh parsley. Serve with pasta or crusty bread.

Quinoa and Avocado Salad

Ingredients:

- 1 cup cooked quinoa
- 1 avocado, diced
- 1/2 cup cherry tomatoes, halved
- 1/4 cup cucumber, diced
- 1 tbsp olive oil
- 1 tbsp lemon juice
- Salt and pepper to taste
- Fresh parsley or cilantro for garnish

Instructions:

In a bowl, mix the cooked quinoa, avocado, cherry tomatoes, and cucumber. Drizzle with olive oil and lemon juice, and season with salt and pepper. Toss to combine and garnish with fresh parsley or cilantro.

One-Pot Pasta Primavera

Ingredients:

- 12 oz pasta (penne or rotini)
- 1 zucchini, sliced
- 1 bell pepper, sliced
- 1 cup cherry tomatoes, halved
- 1/2 cup peas
- 3 garlic cloves, minced
- 2 cups vegetable broth
- 1/2 cup heavy cream
- 1/4 cup grated Parmesan
- Salt and pepper to taste

Instructions:

In a large pot, combine pasta, zucchini, bell pepper, cherry tomatoes, peas, garlic, and vegetable broth. Bring to a boil, then reduce to a simmer. Cook for about 10 minutes until the pasta is tender and most of the liquid is absorbed. Stir in heavy cream, Parmesan, salt, and pepper. Cook for an additional 2 minutes until creamy. Serve immediately.

Teriyaki Chicken Stir-Fry

Ingredients:

- 2 chicken breasts, sliced into thin strips
- 1 bell pepper, sliced
- 1 cup broccoli florets
- 1/4 cup teriyaki sauce
- 1 tbsp sesame oil
- 1 tbsp soy sauce
- 1 tsp sesame seeds (optional)

Instructions:

Heat sesame oil in a large pan over medium heat. Add the chicken strips and cook until browned, about 5 minutes. Add the bell pepper and broccoli, cooking for another 5 minutes. Pour in the teriyaki sauce and soy sauce, tossing to coat the chicken and veggies. Cook for an additional 2-3 minutes. Garnish with sesame seeds if desired, and serve with rice or noodles.

Baked Sweet Potato with Toppings

Ingredients:

- 4 medium sweet potatoes
- 1 cup black beans, drained and rinsed
- 1/2 cup corn
- 1/2 cup diced tomatoes
- 1 avocado, diced
- 1/4 cup Greek yogurt or sour cream
- 1 lime, juiced
- Salt and pepper to taste
- Fresh cilantro for garnish (optional)

Instructions:

Preheat the oven to 400°F (200°C). Pierce each sweet potato several times with a fork and bake for 45-60 minutes until tender. Once cooked, cut them open and fluff the insides with a fork. Top with black beans, corn, diced tomatoes, avocado, Greek yogurt, lime juice, salt, and pepper. Garnish with fresh cilantro if desired.

Pesto Zucchini Noodles

Ingredients:

- 4 medium zucchinis, spiralized
- 1/2 cup pesto
- 1 tbsp olive oil
- 1/4 cup cherry tomatoes, halved
- 1/4 cup grated Parmesan cheese
- Salt and pepper to taste

Instructions:

Heat olive oil in a large skillet over medium heat. Add the spiralized zucchini and cook for 2-3 minutes until just tender. Remove from heat and stir in the pesto, cherry tomatoes, salt, and pepper. Serve warm, topped with grated Parmesan cheese.

Chicken Caesar Salad

Ingredients:

- 2 cups romaine lettuce, chopped
- 1 cup cooked chicken, shredded
- 1/2 cup Caesar dressing
- 1/4 cup croutons
- 1/4 cup grated Parmesan cheese
- Freshly ground black pepper to taste

Instructions:

In a large bowl, combine the chopped romaine lettuce, shredded chicken, and Caesar dressing. Toss to coat evenly. Top with croutons, grated Parmesan cheese, and freshly ground black pepper. Serve immediately.

Classic Tuna Salad Sandwich

Ingredients:

- 1 can (5 oz) tuna, drained
- 1/4 cup mayonnaise
- 1 tbsp Dijon mustard
- 1/4 cup celery, chopped
- 1/4 cup onion, diced
- Salt and pepper to taste
- 4 slices of bread
- Lettuce leaves (optional)

Instructions:

In a bowl, mix together the drained tuna, mayonnaise, Dijon mustard, celery, onion, salt, and pepper until well combined. Spread the tuna salad on two slices of bread, top with lettuce if desired, and place the remaining slices on top. Cut in half and serve.

Egg Fried Rice

Ingredients:

- 2 cups cooked rice (preferably day-old)
- 2 eggs, beaten
- 1 cup mixed vegetables (carrots, peas, corn)
- 3 green onions, chopped
- 2 tbsp soy sauce
- 1 tbsp sesame oil
- Salt and pepper to taste

Instructions:

Heat sesame oil in a large skillet or wok over medium heat. Add the beaten eggs and scramble until fully cooked. Remove from the pan and set aside. In the same skillet, add mixed vegetables and cook until tender. Stir in the cooked rice, soy sauce, and scrambled eggs. Season with salt and pepper, and toss to combine. Cook for an additional 2-3 minutes until heated through.

Veggie and Hummus Wrap

Ingredients:

- 1 large tortilla or wrap
- 1/2 cup hummus
- 1/2 cucumber, sliced
- 1/2 bell pepper, sliced
- 1 carrot, grated
- 1/2 avocado, sliced
- Spinach or mixed greens

Instructions:

Spread hummus evenly over the tortilla. Layer with cucumber slices, bell pepper, grated carrot, avocado, and spinach. Roll the tortilla tightly, slice in half, and serve.

One-Skillet Beef and Broccoli

Ingredients:

- 1 lb beef sirloin, sliced thin
- 2 cups broccoli florets
- 1/4 cup soy sauce
- 2 tbsp oyster sauce
- 2 tbsp sesame oil
- 3 garlic cloves, minced
- Cooked rice for serving

Instructions:

Heat sesame oil in a large skillet over medium-high heat. Add the sliced beef and cook until browned, about 3-4 minutes. Add garlic and broccoli, stirring to combine. Pour in soy sauce and oyster sauce, cooking until broccoli is tender (about 5 minutes). Serve hot over cooked rice.

Avocado Toast with Poached Egg

Ingredients:

- 2 slices of bread (whole grain or sourdough)
- 1 ripe avocado
- 2 eggs
- Salt and pepper to taste
- Red pepper flakes (optional)
- Lemon juice (optional)

Instructions:

Toast the bread slices until golden brown. In a small pot, bring water to a simmer and poach the eggs for about 3-4 minutes until the whites are set. Mash the avocado and spread it over the toasted bread. Season with salt, pepper, and lemon juice if desired. Top each slice with a poached egg and sprinkle with red pepper flakes if using.

Chicken and Rice Soup

Ingredients:

- 1 tbsp olive oil
- 1 onion, diced
- 2 carrots, diced
- 2 celery stalks, diced
- 3 garlic cloves, minced
- 6 cups chicken broth
- 2 cups cooked chicken, shredded
- 1 cup cooked rice
- Salt and pepper to taste
- Fresh parsley for garnish (optional)

Instructions:

Heat olive oil in a large pot over medium heat. Add onion, carrots, celery, and garlic, cooking until softened (about 5 minutes). Pour in the chicken broth, bringing it to a boil. Add shredded chicken, cooked rice, salt, and pepper, simmering for 10 minutes. Garnish with fresh parsley if desired and serve warm.

Mushroom Risotto

Ingredients:

- 1 cup Arborio rice
- 4 cups chicken or vegetable broth
- 1 cup mushrooms, sliced
- 1 onion, finely chopped
- 2 garlic cloves, minced
- 1/2 cup white wine (optional)
- 1/2 cup grated Parmesan cheese
- 2 tbsp butter
- Salt and pepper to taste
- Fresh parsley for garnish

Instructions:

In a saucepan, heat the broth and keep it warm over low heat. In a large skillet, melt 1 tbsp of butter and sauté the onions and garlic until translucent. Add the mushrooms and cook until softened. Stir in the Arborio rice and cook for 1-2 minutes until lightly toasted. Pour in the wine and let it evaporate. Gradually add the warm broth, one ladle at a time, stirring frequently until absorbed. Continue this process until the rice is creamy and al dente. Stir in the remaining butter and Parmesan cheese. Season with salt and pepper, and garnish with fresh parsley before serving.

Turkey and Swiss Quesadilla

Ingredients:

- 4 flour tortillas
- 1 cup cooked turkey, shredded
- 1 cup Swiss cheese, shredded
- 1/2 cup spinach, chopped
- 1 tbsp olive oil
- Salsa and sour cream for serving

Instructions:

Heat olive oil in a skillet over medium heat. Place one tortilla in the skillet and layer with turkey, Swiss cheese, and spinach. Top with another tortilla and cook for 2-3 minutes until the bottom is golden brown. Flip and cook for an additional 2-3 minutes until the cheese is melted. Remove from the skillet, cut into wedges, and serve with salsa and sour cream.

Grilled Chicken with Mixed Greens

Ingredients:

- 2 chicken breasts
- 4 cups mixed greens (spinach, arugula, romaine)
- 1/2 cup cherry tomatoes, halved
- 1/4 cup cucumber, sliced
- 1/4 cup feta cheese, crumbled
- 3 tbsp olive oil
- 2 tbsp balsamic vinegar
- Salt and pepper to taste

Instructions:

Preheat the grill to medium-high heat. Season chicken breasts with olive oil, salt, and pepper. Grill for about 6-7 minutes on each side until cooked through. Remove from the grill and let rest. In a large bowl, combine mixed greens, cherry tomatoes, cucumber, and feta cheese. Slice the grilled chicken and place on top of the salad. Drizzle with balsamic vinegar and additional olive oil before serving.

Homemade Mac and Cheese

Ingredients:

- 8 oz elbow macaroni
- 2 cups cheddar cheese, shredded
- 1/2 cup milk
- 1/4 cup butter
- 1/4 cup all-purpose flour
- 1/2 tsp mustard powder
- Salt and pepper to taste

Instructions:

Cook the macaroni according to package instructions and drain. In a saucepan, melt butter over medium heat. Stir in flour and mustard powder, cooking for 1 minute. Gradually whisk in milk, stirring until thickened. Remove from heat and stir in cheese until melted. Combine cheese sauce with the cooked macaroni, and season with salt and pepper. Serve hot.

Spinach and Feta Stuffed Chicken

Ingredients:

- 4 chicken breasts
- 1 cup spinach, cooked and chopped
- 1/2 cup feta cheese, crumbled
- 1/4 cup cream cheese, softened
- 1 tbsp olive oil
- Salt and pepper to taste

Instructions:

Preheat the oven to 375°F (190°C). In a bowl, mix cooked spinach, feta cheese, and cream cheese until well combined. Cut a pocket into each chicken breast and stuff with the spinach mixture. Season the outside with salt and pepper. Heat olive oil in a skillet over medium-high heat and sear the chicken for 2-3 minutes on each side. Transfer to a baking dish and bake for 20-25 minutes until cooked through.

Lentil and Vegetable Stew

Ingredients:

- 1 cup lentils, rinsed
- 1 onion, diced
- 2 carrots, diced
- 2 celery stalks, diced
- 3 garlic cloves, minced
- 4 cups vegetable broth
- 1 can (14 oz) diced tomatoes
- 1 tsp thyme
- Salt and pepper to taste

Instructions:

In a large pot, sauté onion, carrots, and celery over medium heat until softened. Add garlic and cook for an additional minute. Stir in lentils, vegetable broth, diced tomatoes, thyme, salt, and pepper. Bring to a boil, then reduce heat and simmer for 30-35 minutes until lentils are tender. Serve warm.

Baked Chicken Parmesan

Ingredients:

- 4 chicken breasts
- 1 cup marinara sauce
- 1 cup mozzarella cheese, shredded
- 1/2 cup grated Parmesan cheese
- 1 cup breadcrumbs
- 1 tsp Italian seasoning
- Salt and pepper to taste

Instructions:

Preheat the oven to 400°F (200°C). Season chicken breasts with salt, pepper, and Italian seasoning. Dip each breast in breadcrumbs, coating evenly, and place in a baking dish. Bake for 20 minutes. Remove from the oven, top each breast with marinara sauce and mozzarella cheese, and sprinkle with Parmesan. Return to the oven and bake for an additional 10-15 minutes until the cheese is melted and bubbly.

Tofu and Vegetable Stir-Fry

Ingredients:

- 14 oz firm tofu, cubed
- 2 cups mixed vegetables (bell peppers, broccoli, carrots)
- 2 tbsp soy sauce
- 1 tbsp sesame oil
- 2 garlic cloves, minced
- Cooked rice for serving

Instructions:

Heat sesame oil in a skillet or wok over medium-high heat. Add cubed tofu and cook until golden brown on all sides. Add garlic and mixed vegetables, stirring until the veggies are tender-crisp. Pour in soy sauce and toss to coat. Serve hot over cooked rice.

Omelette with Mushrooms and Cheese

Ingredients:

- 3 large eggs
- 1/2 cup mushrooms, sliced
- 1/4 cup cheese (cheddar, feta, or your choice), shredded
- 1 tbsp butter
- Salt and pepper to taste
- Fresh herbs (optional)

Instructions:

In a skillet, melt butter over medium heat. Add sliced mushrooms and cook until tender. In a bowl, whisk eggs, and season with salt and pepper. Pour the eggs into the skillet and cook until the edges begin to set. Sprinkle cheese over half of the omelette and fold it in half. Cook for another minute until the cheese melts. Serve hot, garnished with fresh herbs if desired.

BBQ Chicken Salad

Ingredients:

- 2 cups cooked chicken, shredded
- 4 cups mixed greens
- 1/2 cup cherry tomatoes, halved
- 1/4 cup red onion, sliced
- 1/2 cup corn (canned or cooked)
- 1/4 cup BBQ sauce
- 1/4 cup ranch dressing

Instructions:

In a large bowl, combine mixed greens, chicken, cherry tomatoes, red onion, and corn. Drizzle BBQ sauce over the salad and toss to combine. Serve with ranch dressing on the side.

Spicy Peanut Noodles

Ingredients:

- 8 oz spaghetti or rice noodles
- 1/4 cup peanut butter
- 2 tbsp soy sauce
- 1 tbsp sriracha (or to taste)
- 1 tbsp honey or maple syrup
- 1/2 cup shredded carrots
- 2 green onions, sliced
- Chopped peanuts for garnish

Instructions:

Cook noodles according to package instructions, then drain. In a bowl, whisk together peanut butter, soy sauce, sriracha, and honey. Toss the warm noodles with the peanut sauce, shredded carrots, and green onions. Garnish with chopped peanuts before serving.

Sausage and Bell Pepper Skillet

Ingredients:

- 1 lb Italian sausage, sliced
- 1 red bell pepper, sliced
- 1 green bell pepper, sliced
- 1 onion, sliced
- 2 cloves garlic, minced
- 1 tbsp olive oil
- Salt and pepper to taste
- Fresh parsley for garnish

Instructions:

In a skillet, heat olive oil over medium heat. Add sliced sausage and cook until browned. Add bell peppers, onion, and garlic, sautéing until vegetables are tender. Season with salt and pepper. Serve hot, garnished with fresh parsley.

Greek Salad with Grilled Chicken

Ingredients:

- 2 cups mixed greens
- 1 cup grilled chicken, sliced
- 1/2 cup cucumber, diced
- 1/2 cup cherry tomatoes, halved
- 1/4 cup red onion, sliced
- 1/4 cup feta cheese, crumbled
- 2 tbsp olive oil
- 1 tbsp red wine vinegar
- Salt and pepper to taste

Instructions:

In a large bowl, combine mixed greens, grilled chicken, cucumber, cherry tomatoes, red onion, and feta cheese. In a small bowl, whisk together olive oil, red wine vinegar, salt, and pepper. Drizzle the dressing over the salad and toss gently to combine before serving.

Tomato Basil Pasta

Ingredients:

- 8 oz pasta (spaghetti or penne)
- 2 cups cherry tomatoes, halved
- 2 cloves garlic, minced
- 1/4 cup fresh basil, chopped
- 3 tbsp olive oil
- Salt and pepper to taste
- Grated Parmesan cheese for serving

Instructions:

Cook pasta according to package instructions and drain. In a skillet, heat olive oil over medium heat. Add garlic and cook until fragrant, then add cherry tomatoes and cook until softened. Toss in the cooked pasta, fresh basil, salt, and pepper. Serve hot with grated Parmesan cheese.

Cottage Pie for One

Ingredients:

- 1 cup ground beef or lamb
- 1/2 cup carrots, diced
- 1/2 cup peas
- 1/2 onion, diced
- 1 tbsp tomato paste
- 1/2 cup beef broth
- 1 cup mashed potatoes (prepared)
- Salt and pepper to taste

Instructions:

Preheat the oven to 400°F (200°C). In a skillet, brown ground beef or lamb with onion and carrots until cooked through. Stir in tomato paste, peas, and beef broth, cooking until heated. Transfer to a small baking dish and top with mashed potatoes. Bake for 20 minutes until golden brown on top.

Eggplant Parmesan

Ingredients:

- 1 medium eggplant, sliced
- 1 cup marinara sauce
- 1 cup mozzarella cheese, shredded
- 1/2 cup grated Parmesan cheese
- 1 cup breadcrumbs
- 1/4 cup flour
- 2 eggs, beaten
- Olive oil for frying

Instructions:

Preheat the oven to 375°F (190°C). Dip eggplant slices in flour, then in beaten eggs, and coat with breadcrumbs. In a skillet, heat olive oil over medium heat and fry eggplant slices until golden brown on both sides. In a baking dish, layer fried eggplant, marinara sauce, mozzarella, and Parmesan. Repeat layers, finishing with cheese on top. Bake for 25-30 minutes until bubbly and golden.

Garlic Butter Shrimp with Rice

Ingredients:

- 1 lb shrimp, peeled and deveined
- 1 cup rice
- 3 tbsp butter
- 4 cloves garlic, minced
- 1/4 cup chicken broth
- 1 tbsp lemon juice
- Salt and pepper to taste
- Fresh parsley for garnish

Instructions:

Cook rice according to package instructions. In a large skillet, melt butter over medium heat. Add garlic and sauté until fragrant. Add shrimp, cooking until pink and opaque, about 2-3 minutes per side. Pour in chicken broth and lemon juice, stirring to combine. Serve shrimp over rice and garnish with fresh parsley.

Pulled Pork Tacos

Ingredients:

- 1 lb cooked pulled pork
- 8 small corn or flour tortillas
- 1/2 cup BBQ sauce
- 1/2 cup coleslaw
- 1/4 cup diced red onion
- Lime wedges for serving

Instructions:

In a skillet, heat pulled pork with BBQ sauce over medium heat until warmed through. Warm tortillas in a separate skillet. Assemble tacos by placing pulled pork on each tortilla, topping with coleslaw and diced red onion. Serve with lime wedges.

Chickpea Curry

Ingredients:

- 1 can (15 oz) chickpeas, rinsed and drained
- 1 can (14 oz) coconut milk
- 1 onion, diced
- 2 cloves garlic, minced
- 1 tbsp curry powder
- 1 tbsp olive oil
- Salt and pepper to taste
- Fresh cilantro for garnish

Instructions:

In a pot, heat olive oil over medium heat. Sauté onion until translucent, then add garlic and cook for another minute. Stir in curry powder, chickpeas, and coconut milk. Simmer for 15-20 minutes until thickened. Season with salt and pepper and garnish with fresh cilantro before serving.

Mini Meatloaf

Ingredients:

- 1 lb ground beef
- 1/2 cup breadcrumbs
- 1/4 cup ketchup
- 1/4 cup onion, diced
- 1 egg
- Salt and pepper to taste

Instructions:

Preheat the oven to 350°F (175°C). In a bowl, combine ground beef, breadcrumbs, ketchup, onion, egg, salt, and pepper. Form the mixture into small loaves and place in a baking dish. Bake for 25-30 minutes until cooked through. Serve with additional ketchup if desired.

Turkey Chili

Ingredients:

- 1 lb ground turkey
- 1 can (14 oz) diced tomatoes
- 1 can (15 oz) kidney beans, rinsed and drained
- 1 onion, diced
- 2 cloves garlic, minced
- 1 tbsp chili powder
- Salt and pepper to taste

Instructions:

In a pot, brown ground turkey over medium heat. Add onion and garlic, cooking until softened. Stir in diced tomatoes, kidney beans, chili powder, salt, and pepper. Simmer for 20-25 minutes, stirring occasionally. Serve hot.

Baked Cod with Lemon

Ingredients:

- 2 cod fillets
- 2 tbsp olive oil
- 1 lemon, sliced
- 1 tsp garlic powder
- Salt and pepper to taste
- Fresh parsley for garnish

Instructions:

Preheat the oven to 400°F (200°C). Place cod fillets on a baking sheet and drizzle with olive oil. Season with garlic powder, salt, and pepper. Top with lemon slices. Bake for 15-20 minutes until the fish is flaky and cooked through. Garnish with fresh parsley before serving.

Sautéed Brussels Sprouts with Bacon

Ingredients:

- 1 lb Brussels sprouts, halved
- 4 slices bacon, diced
- 1/2 onion, diced
- Salt and pepper to taste

Instructions:

In a skillet, cook diced bacon over medium heat until crispy. Remove bacon and set aside, leaving the drippings in the skillet. Add Brussels sprouts and onion to the skillet, sautéing until tender and caramelized. Season with salt and pepper and stir in the cooked bacon before serving.

Pancakes for One

Ingredients:

- 1/2 cup all-purpose flour
- 1 tbsp sugar
- 1 tsp baking powder
- 1/4 tsp salt
- 1/2 cup milk
- 1 egg
- 1 tbsp melted butter
- Maple syrup for serving

Instructions:

In a bowl, whisk together flour, sugar, baking powder, and salt. In another bowl, mix milk, egg, and melted butter. Combine wet and dry ingredients until just mixed. Heat a skillet over medium heat and pour in batter to form a pancake. Cook until bubbles form, then flip and cook until golden brown. Serve warm with maple syrup.

Grilled Veggie Sandwich

Ingredients:

- 1 zucchini, sliced
- 1 bell pepper, sliced
- 1 red onion, sliced
- 1 cup mushrooms, sliced
- 2 tbsp olive oil
- Salt and pepper to taste
- 4 slices whole-grain bread
- 4 oz goat cheese or mozzarella cheese
- Fresh basil leaves (optional)

Instructions:

Preheat a grill or grill pan over medium heat. Toss the sliced vegetables in olive oil, salt, and pepper. Grill the veggies until tender and slightly charred, about 5-7 minutes. Assemble the sandwich by layering grilled veggies and cheese between slices of bread. Toast the sandwich on the grill until the bread is golden brown and the cheese melts. Serve warm, garnished with fresh basil if desired.

Creamy Chicken Alfredo

Ingredients:

- 8 oz fettuccine pasta
- 1 lb chicken breast, diced
- 2 cups heavy cream
- 1/2 cup grated Parmesan cheese
- 4 cloves garlic, minced
- 2 tbsp olive oil
- Salt and pepper to taste
- Fresh parsley for garnish

Instructions:

Cook fettuccine according to package instructions and drain. In a skillet, heat olive oil over medium heat. Add diced chicken and cook until browned and cooked through. Stir in garlic and sauté for another minute. Pour in heavy cream and bring to a simmer, then stir in Parmesan cheese until melted. Add cooked fettuccine to the skillet, tossing to coat. Season with salt and pepper, and garnish with fresh parsley before serving.

Spinach and Ricotta Stuffed Peppers

Ingredients:

- 4 bell peppers, halved and seeded
- 1 cup ricotta cheese
- 2 cups fresh spinach, chopped
- 1/2 cup grated Parmesan cheese
- 1 tsp Italian seasoning
- Salt and pepper to taste
- Marinara sauce for serving

Instructions:

Preheat the oven to 375°F (190°C). In a bowl, mix ricotta cheese, chopped spinach, Parmesan cheese, Italian seasoning, salt, and pepper. Stuff each bell pepper half with the cheese mixture. Place stuffed peppers in a baking dish and cover with foil. Bake for 25-30 minutes until peppers are tender. Serve with marinara sauce.

Steak and Potato Skillet

Ingredients:

- 1 lb steak, diced
- 2 cups potatoes, diced
- 1 onion, diced
- 2 tbsp olive oil
- Salt and pepper to taste
- Fresh rosemary or thyme (optional)

Instructions:

In a skillet, heat olive oil over medium heat. Add diced potatoes and cook until golden and tender, about 10-15 minutes. Push potatoes to the side and add diced steak, cooking until browned. Add onion and cook until softened. Season with salt, pepper, and fresh herbs if using. Serve hot.

Broccoli and Cheddar Frittata

Ingredients:

- 6 large eggs
- 1 cup broccoli florets, chopped
- 1/2 cup cheddar cheese, shredded
- 1/4 cup milk
- Salt and pepper to taste
- 1 tbsp olive oil

Instructions:

Preheat the oven to 375°F (190°C). In a bowl, whisk together eggs, milk, salt, and pepper. In an oven-safe skillet, heat olive oil over medium heat. Add chopped broccoli and sauté until tender. Pour the egg mixture over the broccoli, and sprinkle with cheddar cheese. Cook on the stovetop for 2-3 minutes until the edges begin to set. Transfer the skillet to the oven and bake for 15-20 minutes until the frittata is set and golden. Slice and serve warm.

www.ingramcontent.com/pod-product-compliance
Lightning Source LLC
LaVergne TN
LVHW081503060526
838201LV00056BA/2907

9798330484294